The Usborne
Sleepover Cookbook

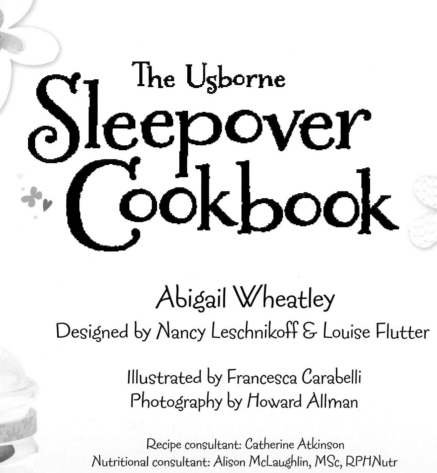

The Usborne
Sleepover
Cookbook

Abigail Wheatley

Designed by Nancy Leschnikoff & Louise Flutter

Illustrated by Francesca Carabelli
Photography by Howard Allman

Recipe consultant: Catherine Atkinson
Nutritional consultant: Alison McLaughlin, MSc, RPHNutr

Contents

How to use this book

Before you start cooking, read the next few pages to get to grips with some cooking basics. Then, check the recipe to see if you have everything you need, wash your hands to make sure you don't spread any germs, and start cooking!

How many?

The recipes in this book are designed for four people — except where it says otherwise. Some are complete meals, but others have suggestions for things that could be served with them.

If you're serving your food in small, party-sized portions, each recipe will serve around eight to ten people, as a light snack.

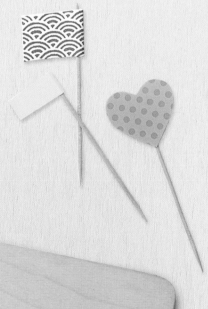

Weighing and measuring

The recipes show two different types of weights. Use either, but don't swap between them. Measure small amounts with spoons, or measuring spoons if you have them.

When you're making cakes or cookies, you need to measure accurately. With other recipes, it doesn't matter so much.

Ingredients should lie level with the top of the spoon.

A pinch is the amount you can pick up between your thumb and first finger.

Salt and spices

Some of the recipes suggest adding a little salt. With others, you don't need to add any as there's enough in other ingredients such as soy sauce or cheese.

None of the recipes in this book is really hot, but some contain a little paprika, chilli, pepper or other spices. If you don't like hot food, reduce the amount you put in, or leave it out altogether. But if you love it, you could add a little more.

Getting started

These tips will help you to get the best out of your cooking equipment, and make sure things always go smoothly when you're in the kitchen.

Oven know-how

Not all ovens are the same, so cooking times may vary. Always check your food is cooked – the recipe will tell you how. And if you have a fan oven, you'll need to shorten the cooking time or lower the temperature a little – your oven manual will tell you how much.

Kitchen kit

If you're using special equipment such as a food processor, make sure you know how to use it. If in doubt, get help from someone who knows how it works.

In the oven

Oven-baked dishes should be cooked in the middle of the oven. Arrange the shelves before you turn on the oven. Set a kitchen timer. Don't keep opening the oven door to check on your food, unless you think something is burning.

Chopping around

When you're cutting with a sharp knife, always use a chopping board. It will stop things from slipping around as you cut them.

Avoiding slip-ups

It's a good idea to wipe up any spills on the floor, so you don't slip on them. If you keep the kitchen tidy as you cook, it will be easier to clean up afterwards.

Too hot to handle

Protect your hands with oven gloves when you handle anything hot, especially when you're getting things in and out of the oven.

Pan handling

If you leave pan handles hanging over the front of your cooker, it's easy to knock them over. Turn handles to the side. And move hot pans carefully, so you don't spill or splash the contents.

All in the timing

Don't leave the kitchen while you've got anything cooking on the stove or under the grill. Set a timer to remind you when to stop cooking. And remember to turn off the heat when you've finished.

Food safety

Meat, especially chicken, can contain nasty bacteria until it's been cooked. Wash your hands, and any dirty knives and chopping boards, as soon as you've finished handling raw meat.

Sleepover snacks

The recipes in this section are designed for sharing. They make ideal sleepover food, because you can eat most of them with your fingers – so everyone can just help themselves.

Pink fizz
– see page 15

Sour cream and chive dip
– see page 10

Baked tortilla chips
– see page 11

Shaped sandwiches
— see page 17

Dips and chips

Here you'll find recipes for some delicious dips, and for baked tortilla chips to dip into them. You could also dip sticks of cucumber, baby corn, celery and red or yellow pepper.

Sour cream and chive dip

Ingredients:

around 25g (1oz) fresh chives
300ml (½ pint) sour cream
1 teaspoon lemon juice

1 Put the chives in a mug. Use kitchen scissors to snip them into tiny pieces. Put 1 tablespoon of chives aside and put the rest in a bowl.

2 Put the sour cream and lemon juice in the bowl. Add a pinch of salt and some pepper. Mix, then sprinkle over the chives you set aside earlier.

Blue cheese dip

To turn the recipe above into a blue cheese dip, you will need 175g (6oz) blue cheese instead of the chives. Remove any rind from the cheese. Mash the cheese with 2 tablespoons of the sour cream, using a fork. You don't need to add any salt. Then, stir in the rest of the sour cream and the lemon juice.

Green pea dip

Ingredients:

250g (9oz) frozen peas
1 lime
1 clove of garlic
½ teaspoon ground cumin
¼ teaspoon ground coriander
100g (4oz) cream cheese, either full-fat or 'light' (avoid 'extra light' types)
a few sprigs of fresh coriander

1 Cook the peas, following the instructions on the packet. Drain them in a sieve, then put them in a large bowl. Use a fork or a potato masher to squash the peas to a lumpy paste.

2 Squeeze the juice from the lime and add it. Crush the garlic into the bowl. Add the cumin, coriander and cream cheese, a pinch of salt and some pepper. Mix.

3 Pick the coriander leaves from the stalks. Put the leaves in a mug and use scissors to snip them into tiny pieces. Mix them in. Eat right away.

If you have a food processor, you can make this dip really smooth. At step 1, just blend the cooked, drained peas to a smooth paste, instead of using a masher.

Paprika dip

Ingredients:

300g (11oz) cream cheese, either full-fat or 'light'
   (avoid 'extra light' types)
1 teaspoon tomato purée
4 tablespoons plain yogurt
2 spring onions
1 large clove of garlic
4 teaspoons mild paprika

1 Put the cream cheese in a bowl. Add the tomato purée and 1 tablespoon of the yogurt. Mix, then add the rest of the yogurt. Mix again.

2 Cut the roots and most of the dark green parts off the spring onions. Slice the rest into very small pieces and put them in the bowl.

Green pea dip

Sour cream and chive dip

Baked tortilla chips

Paprika dip

3 Crush in the garlic, add the paprika, a pinch of salt and some pepper. Stir until well mixed. You could sprinkle a little extra paprika over the top.

Baked tortilla chips

Ingredients:

a little cooking oil
6 corn tortillas weighing about 225g or 8oz in total (gluten-free types are available)

1 Heat the oven to 170°C, 325°F or gas mark 3. Brush around ½ teaspoon of oil over each side of each tortilla. Cut each one into 6 wedges. Spread them over 2 large baking sheets.

2 Bake for 14-15 minutes, until they are golden-brown. Then, take the sheets out of the oven and leave the chips for a minute, to cool and crisp up.

Cheese twists

Ingredients:

- 50g (2oz) hard cheese such as Cheddar or Parmesan
- 100g (4oz) plain flour
- 50g (2oz) butter
- 1 medium egg
- 2 teaspoons poppy seeds (optional)

You will also need a baking sheet, some baking parchment, a pastry brush and a rolling pin.

Makes 12-15 twists

These cheesy pastry twists are crisp and delicious eaten while they're still warm from the oven.

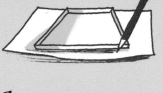

1 Put the baking sheet on the baking parchment. Draw around it. Cut out the shape and put it on the sheet.

2 Grate the cheese on the medium holes of a grater. Sift the flour into a large bowl. Cut the butter into chunks and stir them into the flour.

3 Use the tips of your fingers and thumbs to pick up some butter and flour. Rub them together so they start to mix. The mixed bits will fall back into the bowl. Do this again and again. The lumps of butter will get smaller. Stop when they look like small breadcrumbs.

4 Stir in half the grated cheese. Break the egg into a cup and beat it with a fork. Put two teaspoonfuls of the egg in a cup for later.

5 Stir the rest of the egg into the floury mixture. Squeeze the mixture with your hands until it clings together in a lump.

6 Pat it into a flattened ball, wrap it in plastic food wrap and put it in the fridge for 30 minutes. Meanwhile, heat the oven to 190°C, 375°F or gas mark 5.

7 Sprinkle some flour on a work surface and a rolling pin. Unwrap the dough. Roll the pin over the dough once, then turn the dough a quarter of the way around on the work surface.

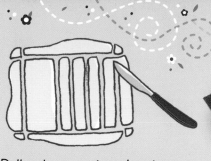

8 Roll and turn again and again, until the dough is about 20cm (8in) square. Cut off the wavy edges, then cut it into about 12 strips.

9 Squeeze the scraps together, roll them out and make more strips. Brush all the strips with the egg you set aside earlier.

10 Scatter the rest of the cheese over the strips, followed by the poppy seeds. Roll the rolling pin over the strips once, lightly.

11 Hold a strip and twist the ends, like this. Put it on the baking sheet and press the ends down. Do the same with the other strips.

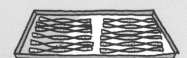

12 Bake for 12 minutes, or until the strips are golden-brown. Leave them on the baking sheet for 5 minutes, then move them to a wire rack to cool.

Other flavours

Instead of poppy seeds, you could use the same amount of sesame seeds. Or, to make slightly spicy twists, sprinkle on 1 teaspoon of paprika.

Pineapple smoothie

Delicious things to drink

All these drinks are quick and easy to make. Each recipe makes 4 ordinary-sized servings, but you could pour them into lots of little glasses instead.

Pineapple smoothie

Ingredients:

2 small bananas

1 lime

1 teaspoon runny honey

150g (5oz) plain yogurt

300ml (½ pint) pineapple juice

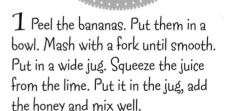

1 Peel the bananas. Put them in a bowl. Mash with a fork until smooth. Put in a wide jug. Squeeze the juice from the lime. Put it in the jug, add the honey and mix well.

2 Add the yogurt and pineapple juice and mix quickly with a fork or whisk, until you have a frothy mixture.

This smoothie tastes extra delicious made with coconut yogurt. Leave out the honey, as coconut yogurt is sweetened already.

Pink fizz

Pink fizz

Ingredients:

50g (2oz) raspberries

100g (4oz) caster sugar

2 lemons

1 litre (1¾ pints) chilled sparkling water

a few ice cubes

1 Put the raspberries in a bowl with the sugar and mash them with a fork until you have a fairly smooth mixture.

2 Squeeze the juice from the lemons. Add it to the raspberries. Add 2 tablespoons of cold water and stir until all the sugar dissolves.

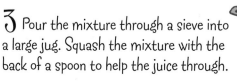

3 Pour the mixture through a sieve into a large jug. Squash the mixture with the back of a spoon to help the juice through.

4 Pour in the fizzy water and add a few ice cubes. Pour it into glasses and drink it right away.

Iced mocha

Ingredients:

4 teaspoons instant coffee, preferably decaffeinated

4 teaspoons cocoa powder

1 tablespoon caster sugar

1 litre (1¾ pints) chilled milk

1 Put the coffee, cocoa and sugar in a mug. Half-fill the mug with very hot water. Stir well, until everything dissolves.

2 Leave to cool for 5 minutes. Then, pour it into a jug, add the milk and stir well. Pour it into glasses.

Iced mocha

For a special treat, you could float a scoop of ice cream on top of your iced mocha.

Little sandwiches

Here you'll find lots of ideas for little sandwiches that are pretty enough for a sleepover, and quick and easy to make, too.

Decorate your sandwiches with paper flags, snipped up cress and chives.

For a double-decker sandwich, make a normal sandwich, then add another layer of filling and an extra slice of bread.

You could cut a hole in the bread for the top of a shaped sandwich, using a tiny cutter.

Spiral sandwiches

Keep them fresh

Sandwiches can go stale quickly if they're left lying around. Eat them right away, or wrap them tightly in plastic food wrap and store them in the fridge.

Finger sandwiches

Ingredients:

8 slices of bread

some butter, margarine or dairy-free spread

sandwich fillings

1 Spread some butter, margarine or spread over each slice of bread. Spread filling over half of them. Put the other slices on top and press down gently.

2 Use a sharp knife to trim off the crusts. Cut each sandwich in half, then cut each half into three finger shapes, like this.

Spiral sandwiches

Ingredients:

8 slices of bread

some butter, margarine or dairy-free spread

sandwich fillings — soft, sticky ones work best here

You will also need a rolling pin.

1 Roll a rolling pin over each slice of bread a few times. Use a sharp knife to trim off the crusts. Spread butter, margarine or spread over each slice.

2 Spread on a thin layer of filling on each slice. Then, roll up each slice into a sausage shape. Cut each one into three pieces.

Shaped sandwiches

Ingredients:

8 slices of bread

some butter, margarine or dairy-free spread

sandwich fillings

You will also need a shaped cookie cutter.

1 Use your cookie cutter to cut as many shapes as you can from each piece of bread, avoiding the crusts. Spread butter, margarine or spread over all the shapes.

2 Spread on any spreadable fillings,  or, if you're using fillings such as ham, smoked salmon or lettuce, put the cutter over the filling and cut around it with a sharp knife.

3 Put fillings on half the shapes. Make sure they don't go over the edges of the bread. Put the rest of the shapes on top and press down gently.

Sandwich fillings

You could use any combination of these filling ingredients in your sandwiches — and add your own favourite fillings, too.

- ☆ cream cheese
- ☆ sliced cucumber
- ☆ jam
- ☆ sliced or grated cheese
- ☆ sliced tomato
- ☆ ham

- ☆ lettuce
- ☆ prawns in pink mayonnaise (page 23)
- ☆ smoked salmon
- ☆ chocolate spread
- ☆ peanut butter

- ☆ salad cress
- ☆ grated carrot with mayonnaise
- ☆ cooled scrambled egg (page 30)

Tiny pizzas

Ingredients:

For the tomato sauce:

2 cloves of garlic

1 tablespoon olive oil

a 400g (14oz) can chopped tomatoes

2 tablespoons tomato purée

1 pinch caster sugar

½ teaspoon dried oregano

For the pizza bases:

225g (8oz) self-raising flour

½ teaspoon baking powder

150ml (¼ pint) milk

1 tablespoon olive oil

For the toppings:

75g (3oz) cheese such as Cheddar or mozzarella (optional)

toppings such as the ones on the page opposite

You will also need a large baking tray, an 8cm (3in) round cookie cutter and a rolling pin.

Makes 10-12

These tiny pizzas make a great sleepover snack, or you could eat two or three of them with some salad for lunch or supper.

1 To make the tomato sauce, crush the garlic into a saucepan. Add the oil, tomatoes, tomato purée, sugar, oregano, a pinch of salt and some pepper.

2 Put the pan over a medium heat and cook for 15 minutes, stirring often, until it is really thick. Leave to cool.

3 Heat the oven to 200°C, 400°F or gas mark 6. Then make the pizza bases. Sift the flour and baking powder into a large bowl. Add the milk and olive oil and mix them in until everything clings together. Pat it into a ball.

4 Sprinkle some flour on a work surface and a rolling pin. Put the dough on the surface and roll it out until it's ½cm (¼in) thick.

5 Use a paper towel to wipe a teaspoon of cooking oil over the baking tray. Use the cutter to cut lots of circles from the dough. Put them on the tray.

6 Squeeze the scraps of dough together, roll them out again and cut more circles. Keep doing this until the dough is used up.

7 Spread a little tomato sauce over each circle (you will only need about half – save the rest for another day). Then grate or slice the cheese and arrange it over the sauce.

8 Add any other toppings. Bake for 10 minutes, or until the bases are risen and golden and the cheese is bubbling. Then, scatter over any fresh herbs or rocket.

Topping ideas

You could use any combination of these topping ingredients on your pizzas – or add your own favourite ingredients.

- ☆ sliced tomatoes
- ☆ black olives
- ☆ ham
- ☆ thinly sliced onion
- ☆ sliced red or yellow pepper
- ☆ feta or other types of cheese
- ☆ pine nuts
- ☆ fresh basil or other herbs
- ☆ pepperoni
- ☆ fresh rocket leaves
- ☆ sliced mushrooms
- ☆ jalapeño peppers from a jar

Sliced red and yellow peppers with rocket

Mozzarella cheese, sliced tomato and fresh basil leaves

Italian ham (prosciutto) and sliced mushrooms

Feta cheese goes well with red onion and fresh thyme.

This pizza is topped with pepperoni and black olives.

Crostini

This recipe is for little toasts called crostini, piled with a fresh tomato and basil topping. You'll find other toppings on the opposite page, too. Crostini make a great snack for sharing.

Ingredients:

For the crostini:
1 loaf of ciabatta bread
1 large clove of garlic

For the tomato topping:
2 tablespoons olive oil
2 teaspoons balsamic vinegar
8 large, fresh basil leaves
8 ripe tomatoes

1 Carefully, cut the loaf into slices about 1cm (½in) thick. Toast in a toaster on a low setting, until golden-brown.

2 Leave the toast to cool. Then, cut the clove of garlic in half. Rub the cut side over one side of each slice of toast.

3 Put the olive oil and vinegar in a bowl with a little pepper and mix. Tear up the basil leaves. Add them, too.

4 Cut the tomatoes into quarters, then into small pieces. Put them in the bowl and mix them in. Spoon the mixture onto the toast and eat right away.

Cut out the green cores.

Sometimes you can get roasted yellow peppers, too.

Mushroom topping

Red pepper topping

Ingredients:

½ x 450g (1lb) jar roasted red or yellow peppers

1 tablespoon olive oil

2 teaspoons lemon juice

100g (4oz) feta cheese

1 Follow steps 1-2 on the opposite page, to make the toasts. Then, rinse the peppers in cold water and leave to drain.

2 Put the olive oil and lemon juice in a bowl. Mix with a fork. Cut the peppers into thin slices. Put them in the bowl and mix well.

3 Spoon the peppers onto the toasts. Crumble the feta into the bowl. Add some black pepper. Stir, then scatter over the crostini.

Mushroom topping

Ingredients:

350g (12oz) mushrooms

15g (½oz) butter

2 teaspoons olive oil

1 large clove of garlic

2 tablespoons crème fraiche or sour cream

1 Follow steps 1-2 on the opposite page. Wipe and slice the mushrooms. Put the butter and oil in a frying pan over a medium heat. When the butter melts, add the mushrooms.

2 Cook, stirring now and then, for 8-10 minutes. Crush in the garlic. Cook for 1-2 minutes, stirring all the time. Stir in the crème fraiche or sour cream. Spoon onto the toasts.

Tomato topping

Salads to share

Here you'll find instructions for preparing salad ingredients, and recipes for salads you can eat for lunch or supper, or as a sleepover snack served in lettuce 'bowls'.

Preparing lettuce

Pull off the leaves. Rinse in cold water, put in a clean tea towel, gather all the edges together and shake it over the sink.

Cutting tomatoes

Cut big tomatoes into quarters, cut the green core from each quarter, then cut the quarters into small pieces, if you like.

Cutting cucumber

Cut the end off the cucumber. Cut the cucumber in half along its length. Cut the halves into quarters the same way. Cut the quarters into slices.

Greek salad

Ingredients:

½ large cucumber
350g (12oz) ripe tomatoes
½ red onion
200g (7oz) feta cheese
75g (3oz) stoned black olives
   (optional)

You will also need the
   dressing below.

1 Cut the half cucumber into slices, and cut the tomatoes into small pieces (see above). Cut the half onion into very thin slices. Chop the slices into small pieces.

2 Put the cucumber, tomatoes and onion in a big bowl. Drain the salty liquid from the feta. Crumble the feta into the bowl.

Vinaigrette dressing

You will need 1 clove of garlic, 4 tablespoons olive oil, 1 tablespoon wine vinegar, 1 teaspoon dried oregano and a jar with a tightly fitting lid. Crush the garlic into the jar. Add the other ingredients. Put on the lid. Shake.

3 Drain the olives. Cut each one into 4 pieces. Put them in the bowl. Pour over the vinaigrette. Mix everything together gently.

Prawn cocktail salad

Ingredients:

½ lemon or lime
2 eating apples
2 ripe avocados
1 cos lettuce, or 2 little gem lettuces
around 250g (9oz) cooked,
    peeled prawns

You will also need the dressing below.

1 Squeeze the juice from the half lemon or lime. Put it in a large bowl. Grate the apples on the large holes of a grater. Put the apple in the bowl and mix.

2 Cut the avocados in half, running the knife around the stone. Scoop out the stones with a spoon. Peel off the skin. Cut the flesh into chunks. Mix them into the apple.

Pink mayonnaise dressing

You will need 2 teaspoons tomato purée, 2 teaspoons lemon or lime juice, 2 tablespoons mayonnaise, 2 tablespoons plain yogurt and ⅛ teaspoon paprika. Put all the dressing ingredients in the cup. Add a pinch of salt and some pepper. Mix well, using a fork.

3 Separate the lettuce leaves, wash and dry them (see opposite). Tear into small pieces and put in the bowl. Mix. Pat the prawns dry with kitchen paper. Put on top of the salad, then drizzle over the dressing.

Prawn cocktail salad in lettuce 'bowls'

To make lettuce 'bowls', separate, wash and dry the leaves of 2 little gem lettuces. Fill them with the Greek salad opposite, or the prawn salad above, leaving out the lettuce.

Sushi

Ingredients:

225g (8oz) sushi rice or other short grain rice

For the toppings:

a piece of cucumber around 6cm (2in) long

1 ripe avocado

1 teaspoon lemon juice

a little smoked salmon

a few cooked, peeled prawns

To serve (optional):

soy sauce and wasabi paste (Japanese horseradish)

You will also need a cake tin, baking tray or plastic box around 20 x 20cm (8 x 8in), and some baking parchment.

This recipe is for a simple type of sushi called nigiri sushi, which comes in little rectangles. Here it's topped with vegetables, smoked salmon and cooked prawns, but you could use other toppings too.

1 Put the rice in a sieve and rinse it under a cold tap. Tip it into a small saucepan. Pour over enough water to cover it by 2½cm (1in). Leave for 30 minutes.

2 Meanwhile, put the tin, tray or box on the baking parchment. Draw around the bottom. Cut out the shape and put it in the tin, tray or box.

3 Drain the rice in the sieve. Tip it back into the pan. Pour on 450ml (¾ pint) cold water. Put the pan over a medium heat. When the water bubbles, put on a lid. Turn the heat down to low, so it bubbles very gently.

4 Cook for 8 minutes. Take off the lid. Stir for 1-2 minutes, or until the rice is very thick and sticky. Spoon into the tin or box.

5 Smooth the top with the back of a spoon. Leave to cool for 5 minutes. Then, cover with plastic food wrap. When the rice is cold, put it in the fridge for 30 minutes.

6 Meanwhile, prepare the vegetables. Stand the cucumber on end. Slice downwards to make thin slices. Cut them in half lengthways.

7 Cut the avocado in half, running the knife around the stone. Scoop out the stone with a spoon. Cut the halves into quarters. Peel off the skin. Cut the flesh into thin strips. Mix them with the lemon juice.

Carrot flowers

Cut a large carrot into thin coin-shapes. Cut a flower from each coin using a small flower-shaped cookie cutter.

Chive ties

Put a few long chives in a heatproof dish. Pour boiling water over them. Leave for 5 seconds. Drain, then cover with cold water. Pat them dry, then lay them on a board. Put a piece of topped sushi over each chive, then bring the ends together on top and tie in a double knot. Snip off the ends.

This flower was made from a slice of radish

A chive tie

Soy sauce

Carrot flowers

8 Turn out the rice onto a board and peel off the baking parchment. Wet the blade of a sharp knife and use it to cut the rice into rectangles about 3 x 6cm (1 x 2in).

9 Top some with the sliced cucumber and avocado. Top others with smoked salmon. Trim the toppings with scissors so they fit on top of the rice.

10 Top others with a row of prawns. If you like wasabi, you could put a little dot of it under each prawn, to help hold it in place.

11 Arrange the sushi on a plate. Put some soy sauce and wasabi in separate little bowls, for people to add to their sushi if they like.

Sticky chicken

Ingredients:

8 chicken drumsticks or thighs, or 16 chicken wings

3 cloves of garlic

2 tablespoons sunflower oil

2 tablespoons soy sauce

2 tablespoons balsamic vinegar

4 tablespoons runny honey

4 teaspoons Chinese five-spice powder (if you can't get this, use 2 teaspoons ground cinnamon and 2 teaspoons ground ginger instead)

You will also need a roasting tray and some kitchen foil.

Pieces of chicken baked in a sticky soy sauce and honey glaze make tasty finger food for sleepovers – but provide plenty of paper napkins. If you're using drumsticks or thighs, you might want to take the skin off them first.

1 Use some paper towel to pat the chicken dry. Use a sharp knife to cut 2 or 3 slashes in each drumstick or thigh. Put the chicken in a shallow bowl. Wash your hands well.

2 Crush the garlic into a small bowl. Add the oil, soy sauce, vinegar, honey, and five-spice powder. Use a fork to mix them together.

3 Pour half the mixture over the chicken, then mix the chicken around to coat it all over. Cover the dish with plastic food wrap. Leave it at room temperature for 15 minutes.

4 Meanwhile, heat the oven to 190°C, 375°F or gas mark 5 and line the roasting tray with kitchen foil. Then, put in the chicken pieces, spacing them well apart.

5 If you're cooking drumsticks or thighs, bake for 25 minutes; if you're cooking wings, bake for 10 minutes. Then, take the tray out of the oven. Turn over the chicken and brush half the remaining soy sauce mixture over it.

6 Bake for 10 minutes more. Then, take the tray out of the oven again. Turn over the chicken and brush the rest of the soy sauce mixture over it. Bake for another 10 minutes.

7 To see if the chicken is cooked, cut into the thickest part with a sharp knife. The meat should be whitish brown. If you can see any pink meat or juices, cook for 10 minutes more, then test again.

Peri-peri chicken

For a peri-peri style sauce, you will need 2 cloves of garlic, 1 tablespoon ground paprika, 2 teaspoons mild chilli powder, 1 teaspoon light soft brown sugar and 1 lime.
Crush the garlic into a bowl. Add the paprika, chilli powder and sugar. Squeeze the juice from the lime and add that too. Brush all of the mixture over the chicken at step 3. Follow step 4, then cook thighs or drumsticks for 45 minutes, wings for 30 minutes.

Meals to share

This section is full of tasty recipes that are great for sharing at sleepovers, or anytime you feel like cooking for friends or family.

Soup in a cup
– see page 32

Fajitas
– see page 36

Delicious things to do with eggs

Eggs are an important ingredient in cooking both sweet and savoury dishes. Here are some tips about how to cook with eggs, and a recipe for French toast – a delicious snack made by dipping bread in egg and frying it until it's crisp and golden. It makes a great breakfast treat.

Storing eggs

If you keep your eggs in the fridge, take them out about an hour before you start cooking. Many recipes work better with eggs at room temperature.

Breaking eggs

Crack the egg sharply on the edge of a bowl. Pull the shell apart, so the white and yolk slide into the bowl. Pick out any bits of shell that fall in.

Beating eggs

Beat the yolk and white quickly with a fork, to mix them together.

Scrambling eggs

1 Allow 1-2 eggs per person. Break them into a bowl. Add 1 tablespoon of milk per person, a pinch of salt and some pepper. Beat with a fork to mix.

2 Put a small chunk of butter in a pan. Put the pan over a medium heat. When the butter melts, pour in the eggs.

3 Stir for 2-3 minutes, until they set into fluffy clusters. Eat straight away on some hot buttered toast.

French toast

Ingredients:

2 medium eggs
75ml (3floz) milk
25g (1oz) butter
1 tablespoon cooking oil
4 thick slices of bread
a little honey, golden syrup
  or maple syrup

1 Break the eggs into a shallow dish. Add the milk and beat with a fork.

2 Heat half the butter and oil in a frying pan over a medium heat for 1 minute, until the butter melts.

3 Dip a slice of bread in the egg mixture, making sure both sides are covered. Put it in the pan. Do the same with a second slice.

4 Cook for 2 minutes, then turn the toast over. Cook for 2 minutes more, until both sides are golden brown. Follow steps 2-4 again for the other 2 slices.

5 Cut each slice into 2 triangles and arrange them on 4 plates. Drizzle over a little honey or syrup. Eat right away.

French toast tastes delicious with fresh fruit such as berries.

Soup in a cup

Ingredients:

1 vegetable stock cube

1 onion

1 large sweet potato, about 250g (9oz)

1 tablespoon cooking oil

1 clove of garlic

a 400ml (14floz) can coconut milk (preferably 'light')

1 pinch dried chilli flakes

a 326g (11oz) can sweetcorn in water

1 lime

This sweet potato, coconut milk and sweetcorn soup makes a warming sleepover supper. To make your soup more substantial, you could add some chicken – there are instructions on the page opposite.

1 Put the stock cube in a jug. Pour on 600ml (1 pint) boiling water and stir until it dissolves.

2 Peel the onion, trim off the ends and cut it in half. Cut the halves into thin slices. Then, cut the slices into small pieces.

3 Peel the sweet potato using a vegetable peeler. Then cut it into chunks around 2cm (1in) across.

4 Heat the oil in a saucepan over a medium heat. Then, put the onion in the pan and cook it for 5 minutes, stirring now and then.

5 Crush the garlic into the pan. Cook for 1 more minute, stirring all the time. Put the sweet potato pieces in the pan, pour in the stock and coconut milk and add the chilli flakes.

6 When the soup starts to boil, turn down the heat so it bubbles gently. Put on a lid, leaving a small gap, and cook for 20 minutes. Meanwhile, drain the sweetcorn in a sieve over the sink. When the soup is cooked, take it off the heat and leave it to cool for 20 minutes.

You could scatter some chopped coriander leaves over the top of your soup when you serve it.

7 If you're using a food processor, ladle in the soup and blend until it's smooth, then pour it back into the pan and skip to step 9. If you're not, follow the next step.

8 To blend the soup by hand, pour it into a sieve over a big bowl. Tip the contents of the sieve back into the pan. Mash with a potato masher until the mixture is fairly smooth. Pour the liquid from the bowl back into the pan and mix.

9 Tip the drained sweetcorn into the pan. Put it over a medium heat for 5 minutes, until the soup is piping hot. Cut the lime into 4 wedges. Serve the soup with a wedge of lime to squeeze over it, before you eat it.

Chicken

You could stir in 200g (7oz) cooked, finely shredded chicken at step 9, when you add the sweetcorn —or instead of the sweetcorn.

Spicier soup

If you like your food spicy, add an extra pinch of chilli flakes at step 5.

Ginger

You will need a 6cm (2in) long piece of fresh ginger. To prepare the ginger, cut away the brown skin, then grate the ginger on the small holes of a grater. Add it at the same time as the garlic in step 5.

Stuffed tomatoes

Ingredients:

4 very large tomatoes, or 8
   medium tomatoes

25g (1oz) couscous

1 medium red onion

1 tablespoon olive oil

1 clove of garlic

200g (7oz) feta cheese

1 pinch dried chilli flakes
   (optional)

1 teaspoon dried oregano

You will also need a shallow
ovenproof dish.

Here you can find out how to make baked tomatoes stuffed with couscous and feta cheese. Eat them with some crusty bread and salad leaves.

1 Turn the oven to 180°C, 350°F or gas mark 4. Cut the tops off the tomatoes about 1cm (½in) from the top.

2 Use a spoon to scoop out all the insides. Throw away any tough bits. Put the seeds and juice in a bowl. Stir in the couscous.

If all the filling won't fit in your tomatoes, put the rest in an ovenproof dish. Cover it with kitchen foil and cook and serve it alongside the tomatoes.

3 Arrange the hollowed-out tomatoes in the dish. If they fall over, wedge small scrunched-up pieces of kitchen foil around them, so they stand up.

4 Peel the onion and cut off the ends. Cut the onion in half. Cut the halves into thin slices, then cut the slices into small pieces.

Stir every now and then.

5 Put the oil in a frying pan and put the pan over a medium heat for 1 minute. Add the onions. Cook for 7-10 minutes, until they are soft. Crush in the garlic. Cook for 1 minute more.

6 Tip the couscous into a sieve over the sink to get rid of any excess juice. Meanwhile, drain the salty water off the feta cheese. Chop the cheese into 1cm (½in) chunks.

Other flavours

You could replace the feta cheese with 200g (7oz) chorizo or other spicy salami-style sausage. Chop it into small pieces and add it in just the same way as the feta cheese.

If you like olives, you could add around 12 chopped, stoned ones to the couscous mixture at step 7.

For a fresh, summery flavour, replace the chilli with the finely grated rind of a lemon at step 7.

7 Put the feta, drained couscous, onions, chilli and oregano in a bowl and mix well. Spoon the mixture into the tomatoes, pressing it down firmly.

8 Put the tops back on the tomatoes and bake for 25-30 minutes, or until the tomatoes are tender.

Fajitas

Ingredients:

1 teaspoon ground cumin

1 teaspoon ground coriander

1 teaspoon paprika

1 teaspoon ground cinnamon

1 pinch chilli powder

300-400g (11-14oz) frying or
   stir-frying steak

1 large or 2 medium red onions

1 small red pepper

1 small orange or yellow pepper

8 soft wraps

1 tablespoon cooking oil such as
   sunflower oil

Fajitas are soft wraps folded around a savoury filling. The filling in this recipe is made from spicy beef and red and yellow peppers, but you'll find alternative filling ideas on the opposite page, too.

1 Put the cumin, coriander, paprika, cinnamon and chilli in a bowl. Add a pinch of salt and mix. Cut any white fat off the steak. Cut the steak into thin strips. Stir them into the spices.

2 Peel the onion and cut off the ends. Cut the onion in half, then cut the halves into slices.

3 Cut the tops off the peppers. Pull out all the seeds and white parts. Cut the peppers into strips around ½cm (¼in) wide.

4 Heat the oven to 200°C, 400°F or gas mark 6. Put the wraps on a baking tray, ready to go in the oven later.

5 Put the oil in a frying pan or wok. Put it over a medium heat for 1 minute. Add the steak strips and cook for 5 minutes, stirring all the time.

6 When the strips are brown all over, take them out and put them on a plate. Put the onion and peppers in the pan. Cook for 7 minutes, stirring all the time.

7 Put the wraps in the oven for 5 minutes. Meanwhile, tip the meat back into the pan. Stir it around, to heat it through again.

8 Take the wraps out of the oven. Spoon some of the pepper mixture onto each one, like this.

9 To wrap up the fajitas, fold the bottom half up over the filling, like this

Other flavours

For chicken fajitas, just replace the steak with 4 skinless, boneless chicken breasts.

For bean fajitas, leave out the steak and use a can of refried beans instead. After step 6, heat the beans according to the instructions on the can. Follow the rest of the steps, spooning some of the refried beans onto each wrap before you add the pepper mixture.

10 Fold one side in, then the other side. Wrap a paper napkin around each fajita, to catch any drips as you eat it.

You could stir some chopped coriander leaves into some sour cream to add to your fajita filling.

Delicious things to do with pasta

Here you'll find instructions for cooking pasta, and several ideas for quick and simple sauces to eat with it.

Cooking spaghetti or other pasta

You will need 300g (11oz) spaghetti or other dried pasta.

3 Boil for 8-12 minutes (follow the timings on the packet). To see if it's cooked, rinse a piece in cold water and bite it. It should be tender but not soggy.

1 Half-fill a large saucepan with water and put it over a high heat until it boils. Turn it down so it bubbles gently. Add a pinch of salt.

2 Add the pasta and stir. For spaghetti, hold it in a bunch at one end and put the other end in the water. As it softens, press it into the water. Stir in the ends.

4 When the pasta is cooked, drain it, then tip it back into the pan, add a sauce and stir.

> One of the simplest ways to eat pasta is with grated cheese. Stir about 50g (2oz) into freshly cooked pasta with a little butter, a pinch of salt and some pepper.

Cherry tomato pasta

Ingredients:

300g (11oz) spaghetti or other dried pasta

around 450g (1lb) ripe cherry tomatoes

1 clove of garlic

4 teaspoons olive oil

1 pinch dried chilli flakes (optional)

about 12 large, fresh basil leaves

1 Put the pasta on to cook. Meanwhile, cut the cherry tomatoes in half and peel the clove of garlic.

2 Put the tomatoes in a pan with the olive oil and chilli flakes. Put the pan over a low heat for 5-7 minutes, until the tomatoes are soft and juicy.

3 Crush in the garlic. Cook for 1 minute, then turn off the heat. Mix into your cooked, drained pasta. Tear up the basil leaves and scatter them on top.

> Cherry tomato pasta tastes good topped with some grated Parmesan cheese, or strips of Parmesan shaved off a block using a vegetable peeler. Or, tear a 125g (4½oz) ball of mozzarella into small pieces and mix it gently into the cooked pasta and sauce at step 3.

Lemon spaghetti

Ingredients:

300g (11oz) dried spaghetti or
   other pasta
75g (3oz) Parmesan cheese
1 lemon
15g (½oz) butter
150ml (¼ pint) double cream

1 Put the pasta on to cook. Meanwhile, grate the Parmesan on the small holes of a grater. Grate the rind from the lemon on the small holes of a grater, too.

2 Squeeze the juice from the lemon. Put the rind, juice, butter and cream in a small saucepan.

3 Put the pan over a very low heat. When the butter melts, turn off the heat. Add the Parmesan and some pepper. Mix into your cooked, drained pasta.

Salmon or prawns

Snip 125g (4½oz) smoked salmon into strips with scissors. Stir it into the sauce at the same time as the pasta. Or, add 150g (5oz) cooked peeled prawns to the sauce in step 2, at the same time as the lemon juice, butter and cream.

Fresh herbs

You could sprinkle some chopped fresh parsley leaves, or other chopped fresh herbs, over your lemon spaghetti if you like.

Serve your lemon spaghetti with a little extra lemon rind grated over it, if you like.

Salmon burgers

Ingredients:

1 teaspoon cooking oil

6 sping onions

450g (1lb) skinless, boneless salmon fillets

1 tablespoon wholegrain mustard

1 teaspoon runny honey

1 clove of garlic

½ lemon

You will also need a food processor.

This recipe shows you how to make burgers from fresh salmon, flavoured with honey, mustard and other good things. You can eat them just like an ordinary burger, in a bun or with potato wedges.

Serve your salmon burger with lettuce, slices of red onion, a drizzle of sour cream and a squeeze of lemon juice.

1 Heat the oven to 200°C, 400°F or gas mark 6. Use a paper towel to wipe the cooking oil over a baking tray.

2 Cut off the ends and most of the dark green parts from the spring onions. Cut the rest into small pieces.

3 Run your fingertips all over the salmon. If you feel any bones, pull them out and throw them away. Put the salmon in the food processor. Add the mustard and honey. Crush in the garlic. Add a pinch of salt.

Stop before the mixture becomes smooth.

4 Squeeze the juice from the lemon and add that, too. Put on the lid and blend at a slow speed, until you have a lumpy paste.

5 Scrape the mixture into a bowl and stir in the spring onions. Use the spoon to divide the mixture into 4 clumps. Spoon each clump onto the baking tray.

6 Use a spoon or your fingers to smooth each clump into a round, flat burger shape. Bake for 15 minutes.

7 Take the tray out of the oven. Cut into one of the burgers. The middle should be the same whitish-pink colour as the outside. If it is still a darker pink, bake for 5 minutes more, then test again.

Other flavours

For burgers with an oriental flavour, leave out the lemon juice, mustard and salt and instead use 1 tablespoon soy sauce and a 6cm (2in) long piece of fresh ginger. To prepare the ginger, cut away the brown skin and grate the ginger on the small holes of a grater. These burgers taste good with sweet chilli sauce.

Salmon bites

For a sleepover snack, instead of making full-size burgers, put teaspoons of the burger mixture onto the baking tray. Bake for 7-10 minutes. Serve with a bowl of sour cream or some sweet chilli sauce for dipping.

Chicken burgers

For juicy chicken burgers, replace the salmon with the same weight of skinless, boneless chicken breasts or thighs. You could also make chicken bites following the instructions for salmon bites, above. Before you eat your chicken bites or burgers, check they are white all the way through, with no sign of pink.

Delicious things to do with potatoes

Here are some recipes for different ways to prepare and cook potatoes. For mashed potatoes, you'll probably want to peel the potatoes first. Otherwise, just scrub them, to remove any dirt.

Scrubbing potatoes

Use a stiff brush to scrub the potatoes under a cold tap. Try to get all the dirt off before you cook them.

Peeling potatoes

Hold the potato and scrape it again and again with a vegetable peeler until you have removed all the skin.

Be careful not to scrape your fingers.

Boiling potatoes

You will need 675g (1½lb) potatoes – use large, fluffy potatoes for mashing. Use small, 'new' potatoes for eating as they are, or for potato salads.

1 Scrub the potatoes, or peel them if they're really muddy. Cut any large potatoes into chunks. Put them in a pan of cold water with a pinch of salt.

They're done when the point of a knife slides in easily.

2 Put the pan over a medium heat, until it boils. Reduce the heat so it bubbles gently. Put on a lid. Cook for 15-20 minutes.

Mashing potatoes

Follow the instructions above to boil some large, fluffy potatoes. Then drain them in a sieve and put them back in the pan. Add 25g (1oz) butter, 4 tablespoons of milk, a pinch of salt and some pepper. Mash with a potato masher until no lumps are left. (For a really smooth mash, peel the potatoes first.)

Baked potatoes

You will need 4 big potatoes (or 8 small ones), a little butter, margarine or spread and a topping, such as 200g (7oz) grated hard cheese, or 8 tablespoons of coleslaw, sour cream and chive dip (see page 10) or heated baked beans.

1 Heat the oven to 180°C, 350°F or gas mark 4. Use a fork to prick holes all over the potatoes, then put them on a baking tray. Bake for 1 hour.

2 Wearing oven gloves, squeeze the potatoes gently. If they feel soft, they're ready. If not, cook for another 15 minutes and try again.

3 When they're done, cut a cross in the top of each one. Put a little butter or spread in each one. Add a topping too, if you like.

Spicy potato wedges

Ingredients:

675g (1⅓lb) large potatoes,
   preferably ones suitable for
   baking, such as Maris Piper
2 tablespoons cooking oil,
   such as sunflower oil
1 teaspoon paprika
1 pinch chilli powder

1 Heat the oven to
200°C, 400°F or gas
mark 6. Scrub the
potatoes, or peel them
if they're very muddy.

*Spicy wedges taste good
with tomato ketchup.*

2 Cut the potatoes in half, then cut the
halves into wedges that are all about the
same size. Try to make sure they're no
thicker than around 2cm (1in).

*They're done when they're
soft in the middle and golden.*

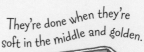

3 Put the oil on a baking tray.
Tumble the wedges around to
coat them in the oil. Cook for
20-30 minutes.

4 Mix the paprika, chilli and a pinch
of salt in a small bowl. Sprinkle it over
the wedges. Turn the wedges with a
spatula to coat them in the spice mix.

Potato salad

Follow the instructions on the opposite page to boil some small, new potatoes. Drain in a sieve and
leave to cool. Meanwhile, chop the pale parts of 4 spring onions and mix with 1 tablespoon lemon
juice, 3 tablespoons mayonnaise and 4 tablespoons plain yogurt. Add the potatoes and mix gently.

Sweet treats

The recipes in this section are full of sugar and spice and all things nice, perfect for sleepover desserts – or delicious treats for any occasion.

Flower cupcakes – see page 58

Cinnamon cookies – see page 48

Raspberry swirl cake – see page 56

Chocolate fondue

Ingredients:

around 450g (1lb) fresh fruit for dipping, such as berries, grapes, cherries, apples or bananas

200g (7oz) plain chocolate

150ml (¼ pint) double cream

2 teaspoons runny honey

You will also need some skewers or cocktail sticks.

If you're dipping bananas or apples, you'll need some lemon juice, too.

This luscious chocolate fondue makes a great sleepover pudding. Put out lots of fresh fruit for everyone to dip into it, and give it a stir every now and then to keep it silky and smooth.

1 First, prepare the fruit. If you're using berries, cherries or grapes, put them in a sieve and wash them in cold water. Pull any grapes off their stalks.

2 Cut any apples into quarters, remove the cores, then cut the apple into bite-sized pieces. Peel any bananas and cut them into bite-sized pieces.

3 Put the apple or banana pieces in a bowl. Add half a teaspoon of lemon juice per apple or banana and mix to coat the fruit in the juice. This will stop it from going brown.

4 Leave any fruits with stalks, such as strawberries or cherries. Push other pieces of fruit onto skewers or cocktail sticks. Arrange the fruit in bowls or on plates.

5 Break the chocolate into small chunks. Put the cream and honey in a small saucepan.

6 Put the pan over a medium heat. Leave it until the cream steams and small bubbles form around the edge. Take the pan off the heat.

Marshmallows are good to dip, too.

7 Stir in the chocolate until it melts and you have a smooth mixture. Then, pour it into a bowl. Eat it straight away.

Other flavours

You can replace the plain chocolate with milk chocolate. But leave out the honey, as milk chocolate is sweet enough already.

Other fruit

Tangerines are good for dipping. Peel them and separate out the segments.

Instead of fresh fruit, you could use canned fruit such as pineapple chunks, peaches or pears. Drain them first.

Cinnamon cookies

Ingredients:

215g (7½oz) self-raising flour

4 teaspoons ground cinnamon

¼ teaspoon ground black pepper (optional)

50g (2oz) butter

50g (2oz) soft dark brown sugar

3 rounded tablespoons golden syrup or runny honey

You will also need cookie cutters, some writing icing for decorating, two baking sheets and a rolling pin.

These crisp cookies taste deliciously of cinnamon. A little black pepper gives them a hint of spicy warmth, but doesn't actually make them taste peppery. Decorate your cookies with pretty colours of writing icing.

1 Heat the oven to 180°C, 350°F or gas mark 4. Lay the baking sheets on some baking parchment. Draw around them. Cut out the shapes and put them on the sheets.

2 Sift the flour, cinnamon and pepper into a large bowl. Put the butter, sugar and syrup or honey in a pan. Put over a gentle heat, stirring now and then, until the butter has melted.

3 Take the pan off the heat, add the flour and mix until it clings together. Put a lid on the pan and leave for about 5 minutes, to let the mixture cool.

4 Sprinkle a clean surface and rolling pin with flour. Put the dough on the surface. Pat and squash it gently with your hands, until it you have a smooth ball of dough.

5 Put half the dough back in the pan, with the lid on. Sprinkle some flour on a work surface and a rolling pin. Put the other half of the dough on the surface. Roll it out until it is half as thick as a pencil.

6 Cut out lots of shapes using cookie cutters. Put the shapes on the trays. Roll out the other half of the dough. Cut more shapes.

7 Squeeze any scraps of dough together and roll them out again. Cut more shapes. Do this until all the dough is used up.

8 Bake for 8-10 minutes, until the cookies are slightly browned at the edges. Leave on the trays for a few minutes, then move them to a wire rack to cool.

9 When the cookies are completely cool, decorate them with writing icing.

Other flavours

For ginger cookies, replace 3 teaspoons of the cinnamon with ground ginger. Leave out the black pepper, as ginger has its own spicy kick.

For plain vanilla cookies, replace the dark brown sugar with caster sugar and replace the spices with 1 teaspoon vanilla extract.

Fruit jellies

Ingredients:

600ml (1 pint) fruit juice from a carton, such as cranberry, apple or orange

6 leaves of gelatine

1 tablespoon caster sugar (optional)

around 225g (8oz) fresh ripe fruit such as berries, peaches, plums, apricots, pears, apples or grapes

You will also need 4 glasses, bowls or pots.

These jellies are made from fresh fruit and juice, set firm using gelatine. You can use almost any fruit, but there are a few that won't work – there's a list on the opposite page. You will only need to add the sugar if you're using a sour juice such as orange juice.

Sliced apricot

Redcurrants

1 Pour a quarter of the fruit juice into a small saucepan. Cut the gelatine leaves in half with scissors, then put them in the pan. Add the sugar, too. Leave for 5 minutes.

2 The gelatine will now be soft. Put the pan over a medium heat. Stir every now and then, and make sure the mixture doesn't boil.

3 As soon as all the gelatine has dissolved, and there are no strands clinging to the spoon, take the pan off the heat. Pour in the rest of the juice. Stir. Leave to cool.

4 Next, prepare the fruit. Cut up any large berries or grapes, leaving small ones whole. Cut any apples or pears into quarters, then cut out the cores and cut the fruit into bite-sized pieces.

Other flavours

There are so many combinations of juice and fruit you could use for this recipe. You could even buy canned fruit in natural juice – use the juice to make the jelly and top it up with juice from a carton. Here are some ideas for flavour combinations:

☆ grape juice with red and white grapes and blueberries

☆ cranberry juice with blueberries, raspberries and strawberries

☆ orange juice with sliced bananas and tangerine segments

☆ apple and raspberry juice with raspberries and sliced apples and pears

These jellies were made using a mixture of white grape juice and cranberry juice.

5 For fruits with central stones, slide in a knife until the point touches the stone. Move the knife around the fruit, following the stone. Pull the fruit apart, remove the stone and cut up the fruit.

6 Divide the fruit between the dishes, then pour over the jelly. Put the dishes in the fridge for 2 hours, to set.

What not to use

Pineapple, kiwi fruit and papaya all stop gelatine from setting properly.

Avoid using these fruits and juices made from them. If you're thinking of using juice blends such as tropical fruit juices, make sure none of these fruits is included.

Little lime cheesecakes

Ingredients:

350g (12oz) full-fat cream cheese

175g (6oz) digestive biscuits

75g (3oz) butter

3 limes

125g (4½oz) caster sugar

150ml (¼ pint) double cream

You will also need a 12-hole deep muffin tray, 12 paper muffin cases and a rolling pin.

Makes 12

These moist, tangy little cakes are made with cream cheese flavoured with lime zest and juice. They set in the fridge, so they are simple to make, and softer and creamier than baked cheesecakes.

1 Take the cream cheese out of the fridge and leave it at room temperature for half an hour. Put a paper case in each hole of the muffin tray.

2 Put the biscuits in a clean plastic food bag. Seal the end with an elastic band. Roll a rolling pin over it to crush the biscuits into pieces the size of large breadcrumbs.

3 Put the butter in a saucepan and put it over a low heat. When the butter melts, turn off the heat.

4 Add the biscuit crumbs to the butter and mix. Divide the mixture between the paper cases. Press it down well with the back of a teaspoon. Put the tray in the fridge to chill.

Only remove the green layer – the white layer underneath tastes bitter.

5 Grate the rind from the outside of the limes, using the small holes on a grater. Then, cut the limes in half and squeeze out the juice. Put the juice and rind in a mixing bowl. Add the cream cheese, sugar and cream and mix well.

6 Take the tray out of the fridge. Divide the cream cheese mixture between the paper cases. Level the tops with the back of a spoon. Put the tray back in the fridge for at least 2 hours.

Big cheesecake

You can use this recipe to make a big lime cheesecake. Grease and line a 20cm (8in) round cake tin with a loose base, following the instructions in step 1 on page 56. Follow the cheesecake recipe as normal. When the cheesecake has chilled, put the cake tin over a food can. Press the sides of the tin down around the can. Then, slide the cheesecake off the base of the cake tin, onto a plate.

Lime and ginger cheesecakes

Replace the digestive biscuits with ginger biscuits. For extra zing, mix ½ teaspoon ground ginger into the biscuit crumbs at step 4, when you mix them into the butter.

Lemon cheesecakes

For tangy lemon cheesecakes, simply replace the limes with 2 large lemons.

These little curls of lime zest were made by scraping a tool called a zester across the surface of a lime.

Peel off the paper cases before you eat the cheesecakes.

Tangerine ice

Ingredients:

8-10 tangerines

50g (2oz) caster sugar

1 rounded tablespoon golden syrup

½ lemon

You will also need a shallow freezer-proof container with a tightly fitting lid.

This recipe is made from frozen tangerine juice, which is broken into little crystals. This type of dessert is sometimes called 'granita'. It's like a slightly crunchy sorbet, or the icy slush drinks you can buy.

Only remove the orange layer – the white layer underneath tastes bitter.

1 Grate the rind from the outside of one of the tangerines, using the small holes on a grater. If you find it's difficult to grate, use a vegetable peeler to peel off the outer layer of rind instead.

2 Put the rind in a small saucepan with the sugar, syrup and 4 tablespoons of water. Put the pan over a low heat.

3 Stir the mixture every now and then, until the sugar has dissolved. When the mixture starts to bubble, turn off the heat and put on a lid.

Squash the bits in the sieve with the back of a spoon to help the juice through.

4 Cut 8 of the tangerines in half and squeeze out the juice. Squeeze the juice from the half lemon, too. Strain the juice through a sieve into a measuring jug.

5 You need around 250ml (9floz) juice. If you don't have enough, squeeze the juice from the remaining tangerines and add that, too.

6 Pour the cooled sugary mixture through the sieve into the jug. Throw away the bits left in the sieve.

7 Pour the mixture into the freezerproof container and put on the lid. Freeze for 6 hours, or longer if you prefer. To serve, scrape a fork over the top layer, to make a pile of ice crystals. Keep on scraping until all the ice is in crystals. Eat right away.

Other flavours

For orange, lime or lemon ice, you could replace the tangerines with 5 oranges, 8 limes or 6 lemons. Or you could use a mixture of different citrus fruits – just make sure you have 250ml (9floz) juice at step 5.

Raspberry swirl cake

Ingredients:

100g (4oz) butter, softened

100g (4oz) caster sugar

2 medium eggs

1 teaspoon vanilla essence

100g (4oz) self-raising flour

3 tablespoons milk

For the topping:

150g (5oz) fresh raspberries

300ml (½ pint) double cream or whipping cream

50g (2oz) bought meringues

You will also need a 20cm (8in) cake tin.

This recipe is for a vanilla sponge cake, topped with a cloud of whipped cream swirled with crushed meringues and raspberries. You can also make gluten-free raspberry swirl cupcakes, using this topping instead of icing for the cakes on pages 58-59.

1 Heat the oven to 180°C, 350°F or gas mark 4. Dip a paper towel in some softened butter and wipe it around the inside of the cake tin. Put the tin on some baking parchment. Draw around it. Cut out the shape and put it inside the tin.

2 Put the butter and sugar in a large bowl. Beat them very quickly with a spoon, until you have a smooth mixture.

3 Break each egg into a cup, then tip it into a small bowl. Add the vanilla. Beat with a fork to mix it all together. Add a spoonful of the egg mixture to the butter mixture. Beat it in well. Add the rest of the egg a spoonful at a time, beating well each time.

4 Sift the flour through a sieve into the bowl. Mix it in very gently, moving the spoon in the shape of a number 8. Then, add the milk and mix it in gently.

5 Pour and scrape the mixture into the cake tin. Smooth the top with the back of a spoon. Bake for 20 minutes, or until it is risen and golden.

6 Take the cake out of the oven. Poke the middle gently. If it is firm and springs back, it's cooked. If not, bake for 5 minutes more and try again.